HEARING GOD'S VOICE FOR HEALING OFFICIAL WORKBOOK

PRACTICAL PATHS TO DIVINE HEALTH

MARK VIRKLER

PATTI VIRKLER

DESTINY IMAGE

Destiny Image P.O. Box 310, Shippensburg, PA 17257-0310

This book and all other Destiny Image's books are available at Christian bookstores and distributors worldwide.

For Worldwide Distribution.

Reach us on the Internet: www.destinyimage.com.

ISBN 13 TP: 9798881504540

ISBN 13 eBook: 9798881504557

CONTENTS

INTRODUCTION

Welcome to the *Hearing God's Voice for Healing Official Workbook*. This journey is designed to guide you into a deeper understanding of God's heart for healing and how you can actively participate in His work of restoration, not only in your life but also in the lives of others. Healing is more than a miracle or an event; it is a lifestyle, a Spirit-led walk of intimacy with God where His voice becomes the cornerstone of every action, thought, and decision. Through this workbook, you will explore powerful principles, actionable steps, and profound truths that will transform how you engage with God's healing power.

The core of this workbook revolves around one foundational truth: **healing flows from a relationship with God, where we learn to hear His voice and respond in faith and obedience.** Throughout the chapters, you will be immersed in teachings, reflections, and exercises that draw directly from Scripture, allowing you to anchor your faith in God's unchanging Word. Each lesson is a step forward into a life where the miraculous becomes natural and the presence of God permeates every part of your being.

This workbook invites you to examine and apply **the key principles of hearing God's voice for healing**, which can be summarized in the following ways:

ABIDING IN CHRIST IS THE FOUNDATION FOR FRUITFULNESS AND HEALING

- Just as a branch cannot bear fruit unless it remains connected to the vine, we cannot live a life of abundance apart from our connection with Jesus. This workbook will teach you how to remain in Him, moment by moment, and how His Spirit empowers every aspect of your life.

HEALING IS GOVERNED BY SPIRITUAL LAWS THAT ARE ACCESSIBLE THROUGH THE HOLY SPIRIT

- God's Kingdom operates on principles that, when understood and applied, open the door to divine intervention. Whether it is faith, forgiveness, speaking life, or aligning with God's truth, these principles will be unpacked in detail to equip you to walk in divine power.

GOD'S RIVER OF LIFE FLOWS CONTINUOUSLY TO SUSTAIN, HEAL, AND EMPOWER

- This workbook emphasizes the significance of the imagery found in Revelation and Psalms, where the River of Life symbolizes the unending flow of God's Spirit. As you progress, you will learn how to live in this flow, experiencing the fullness of His presence daily.

THE POWER OF WORDS IS VITAL TO RELEASING GOD'S HEALING

- Life and death are in the power of the tongue. This workbook will guide you to align your words with God's promises, speak truth over your circumstances, and partner with the Holy Spirit in declaring His will on earth.

DIVINE HEALING BEGINS WITH COMMUNION AND INTIMACY WITH GOD

- Healing is not a distant reality but a fruit of abiding fellowship with the Creator. This workbook will show you how to cultivate an environment where God's presence becomes your daily reality, transforming your mind, emotions, and body.

HEALING IS BOTH IMMEDIATE AND PROGRESSIVE

- While miracles can happen in a moment, the journey of restoration often unfolds in layers. Through this workbook, you will gain insight into walking through the process of healing with faith and trust, recognizing God's hand in every step.

GOD CALLS US TO BE VESSELS OF HIS HEALING POWER FOR OTHERS

- As you learn to hear His voice, you will discover how to partner with Him in bringing healing to those around you. This workbook equips you to discern His leading, step into boldness, and release His power through prayer, words of knowledge, and acts of compassion.

PICTURES, VISIONS, AND DREAMS ARE ESSENTIAL TOOLS FOR SPIRITUAL TRANSFORMATION

- The eyes of your heart must be fixed on Jesus, and this workbook will show you how to engage your imagination in godly ways, allowing the Holy Spirit to reveal truths and inspire actions that align with His will.

FAITH WORKS THROUGH LOVE AND IS ACTIVATED BY OBEDIENCE.

- True faith is not passive but active, demonstrated through actions that reflect God's heart. This workbook emphasizes the interplay of love and faith, helping you understand how to release God's power through compassionate and Spirit-led actions.

HEALING FLOWS MOST EFFECTIVELY IN UNITY WITH THE BODY OF CHRIST

- Whether it is through corporate prayer, the counsel of spiritual advisors, or shared worship, the power of agreement is central to experiencing the fullness of God's healing. This workbook will encourage you to engage with others in your journey, recognizing the strength that comes from community.

As you move through the chapters, you will encounter reflective questions, journaling prompts, and actionable steps designed to deepen your understanding and sharpen your spiritual sensitivity. These elements are not mere exercises but pathways to encountering God personally. By engaging fully, you will unlock the potential of hearing His voice clearly and consistently, transforming every area of your life.

This workbook is for anyone who desires to experience the reality of God's healing—spirit, soul, and body. It is for the seeker longing to hear God's voice, the believer yearning to walk in greater faith, and the servant ready to be used by God as an instrument of His healing power. Whether you are new to the faith or have walked with God for decades, this journey promises to draw you closer to Him and equip you to live a life that reflects His glory.

Through each chapter, you will find the encouragement to step into the promises of God boldly. You will learn to replace fear with faith, doubt with trust, and self-effort with Spirit-led obedience. The truths within these pages are not abstract concepts but practical realities that, when embraced, will transform how you live and minister.

WHAT CAN YOU EXPECT TO RECEIVE FROM THIS WORKBOOK?

You will receive a greater awareness of God's voice in your life, a deeper understanding of the principles of healing, and a renewed passion for abiding in His presence. You will be equipped with the tools to navigate life's challenges with confidence, knowing that His Spirit guides and empowers you. Most importantly, you will discover that healing is not a distant possibility but a present reality available to you today.

As we begin this journey together, let us remember that the goal is not merely to gain knowledge but to experience transformation. God is ready to meet you where you are and take you deeper into His purposes. May this workbook be a tool in His hands to reveal His love, power, and glory in your life.

Welcome to the journey. Let us step into the River of Life, abide in His presence, and bear fruit continually. Together, we will learn to hear His voice, experience His healing, and become vessels of His hope to a world in need.

❧

CHAPTER I

TESTIMONIES OF VARIOUS WAYS GOD HEALS

"Behold, I will bring it health and healing; I will heal them and reveal to them the abundance of peace and truth." - Jeremiah 33:6 NKJV

In this journey of understanding how God heals, it is essential to recognize that healing can occur in many forms. **Multiple Modalities of Healing** are evident through the testimonies shared in this chapter, showing that God's intervention is not limited to instantaneous miracles. Sometimes, healing is a gradual process that unfolds over time, much like the story of Uta Milewski, who experienced significant improvement in her health through sustained lifestyle changes. This teaches us that while we may desire quick solutions, God's timing and methods are diverse, and our openness to different healing experiences can deepen our faith and understanding of His care.

In my own experiences and those of others, I've seen how profound the impact of emotional and spiritual states can be on physical health. For example, the story of the young lady with the neck pain highlights the powerful connection between emotional burdens and physical symptoms. Here, **Forgiveness from the Heart** led to healing, underscoring the fact that sometimes, what we need to heal physically is to first address our emotional wounds. This revelation has often come through prayer and reflection, leading to a significant release of pain and an increase in physical well-being.

As we navigate through our healing journeys, it is crucial to **Cooperate with Divine Guidance**. This means staying attuned to God's voice and adhering to the steps He lays out for us. Whether it's adjusting our diet, changing our environment, or altering our exercise routines, these adjustments can be instrumental in our healing processes. God's guidance is not always about doing less; sometimes, it involves doing more or different things that align better with His plans for our health and wholeness.

The process of healing, especially from chronic conditions, often requires gaining **Divine Wisdom** for health. It's not merely about praying for healing but also seeking God's wisdom on how to manage or eliminate the factors contributing to our ailments. My friend Uta's story is a testament to the significant improvements that can occur when we actively seek divine wisdom and make informed health decisions based on that guidance.

Process Healing Through Lifestyle Changes is another critical aspect that we observe, particularly in long-term health battles like chronic illnesses. It's not just about receiving healing but maintaining it through consistent and healthy choices. As seen in Uta's narrative, a journey of small, daily decisions led to substantial improvements in her respiratory health, demonstrating that process healing is often about persistence and gradual progress.

Community has always played a pivotal role in the healing process. The act of coming together to pray for one another, as seen in the church service anecdotes, highlights how **Power of Community Prayer and Support** can lead to miraculous recoveries. These moments of collective faith and intercession are not only uplifting but also instrumental in manifesting God's healing power among His people.

It's intriguing to note how often physical ailments have underlying emotional or spiritual causes. This connection means that to truly heal, one must often delve deeper than the surface symptoms. **Emotional Roots of Physical Illness** need to be identified and addressed, which can lead to profound and lasting healing, as the spirit and body are intricately connected.

For those of us seeking to live a fulfilled and healthy life, learning to **Live by the Spirit** becomes essential. This involves understanding how to discern and follow the Holy Spirit's guidance in every aspect of life, including our health. By mastering this skill, we learn to walk in a manner that aligns with God's will, leading to improved spiritual, emotional, and physical health.

In the realm of spiritual healing, invoking the **Importance of Names of God in Healing** like Jehovah Rapha or Jehovah Shalom can bring significant comfort and power into our healing processes. These names are not just symbolic but are carriers of God's promise for restoration and peace, each reflecting a specific aspect of His ability to heal and sustain us.

Lastly, I have found great value in using **Journaling as a Tool for Healing**. This practice not only allows for an ongoing dialogue with God but also helps in tracking the progress of one's healing journey. Writing down your experiences, feelings, and revelations can provide insights and sustained encouragement, serving as a reminder of God's faithfulness through all stages of healing.

REFLECTIVE QUESTIONS

1. How do I currently view God's role in healing—do I lean more towards expecting instantaneous miracles, or am I open to the idea of process healing?
2. Are there areas of unforgiveness in my life that might be hindering my physical or emotional health?
3. What practical steps can I take to become more in tune with God's guidance regarding my health?
4. How can I incorporate seeking divine wisdom into my daily routine to make better health decisions?
5. What does living by the Spirit look like in my current context, and how can I cultivate this practice daily?

ACTIONABLE STEPS

- **Cultivate a Regular Prayer Routine**: Establish a daily prayer routine where you seek God's guidance for health and healing. Use this time to surrender your health issues and ask for wisdom in managing them.
- **Equip Yourself with Knowledge**: Learn about the connections between emotional health and physical symptoms. Equip yourself with tools like journaling, counseling, and spiritual teachings that address these aspects.
- **Engage in Community Support**: Actively seek and participate in prayer groups or healing ministries. Engage in community support not just for your own healing, but also to pray for and support others in their health journeys.

. . .

Journaling **Prompt**

Reflect on the recent times you've experienced healing, whether instant or over a period. What were the circumstances, and how did you see God's hand at work? How can these experiences shape your understanding of God's healing power in your life?

CHAPTER 2

INSTANTANEOUS MIRACLES VERSUS PROCESS HEALING

"Behold, I am the Lord, the God of all flesh. Is there anything too hard for Me?" - Jeremiah 32:27 NKJV

In our exploration of God's manifold ways of healing, it becomes clear that the divine operates through both **Instantaneous Miracles and Process Healing**. These methods reveal the breadth and depth of God's engagement with our physical and spiritual well-being. Instantaneous miracles are those awe-inspiring moments when healing occurs in the blink of an eye, often defying medical explanations and serving as powerful testimonies of God's immediate presence and power. However, process healing invites us into a journey, a step-by-step recovery where our faith is stretched and our understanding deepened.

In diving into the Scriptures, we encounter the Greek words **dunamis** and **semeion**, which enrich our understanding of miracles. The word **dunamis** refers to "power," suggesting a dynamic and transformative force, while **semeion** means "sign," pointing beyond itself to divine truths. These terms help us see miracles not just as acts of power but as signs that guide us to a deeper recognition of God's sovereignty and the reality of His kingdom among us.

The two primary Greek words translated as "healing" in the New Testament are **iaomai** and **therapeuo. Iaomai** is often used in the context of instant healing, a sudden restoration that showcases God's power. Conversely, **therapeuo** implies a therapeutic process, involving more gradual healing that may include medical treatment, lifestyle adjustments, and ongoing spiritual care. This distinction is crucial for understanding the full spectrum of healing that the Bible presents.

Adding another layer to our understanding of biblical healing practices are methods like **Anointing with Oil** and the use of **Herbal Remedies**. These practices, rooted in ancient traditions and supported by scriptural references, illustrate the holistic approach God endorses for our healing. Anointing with oil, for example, has been a symbol of the Holy Spirit's presence and a conduit of divine blessing and healing throughout the ages.

Similarly, the practice of **Laying on of Hands** is predominantly associated with therapeuo healing in the Scriptures. This act not only signifies a physical point of contact but also represents a spiritual connection and transfer of God's healing power. It's fascinating to consider how contemporary practices like chiropractic might connect with these ancient traditions, suggesting that physical touch continues to play a vital role in healing.

These insights compel us to appreciate the diversity in the methods through which God heals and to embrace both miraculous and process-oriented healings in our faith communities. By understanding and applying these principles, we can more fully cooperate with God's work in our lives and the lives of others, fostering a deeper and more comprehensive approach to healing that spans both the miraculous and the methodical.

REFLECTIVE QUESTIONS

1. How do I perceive miracles? Do I expect them to be instantaneous, or am I open to the idea of process healing as a form of miraculous intervention?
2. How does understanding the different Greek words for healing change my expectations when praying for healing for myself or others?
3. In what ways can I incorporate natural elements like oil or herbal remedies into my understanding and practice of biblical healing?
4. What role does faith play in my acceptance of both instantaneous miracles and process healing?
5. How can I better support others in their healing journeys, recognizing that their paths might involve either sudden miracles or gradual healing?

ACTIONABLE STEPS

- **Cultivate an Inclusive Understanding of Healing**: Broaden your understanding of what healing can look like. Recognize that both instantaneous and process healings are valid and powerful ways God restores health.
- **Equip with Scriptural and Practical Knowledge**: Study the biblical terms and contexts for healing. Equip yourself with practical knowledge about

natural remedies and prayer practices that align with scriptural insights.

- **Engage in Prayer and Practical Ministry**: Actively engage in praying for others, using both the laying on of hands and anointing with oil where appropriate. Be open to God using you in both miraculous and therapeutic ways to bring healing.

JOURNALING **Prompt**

Reflect on the nature of healing as described in this chapter. Consider the times when you have experienced or witnessed healing, whether instantaneous or gradual. How do these experiences shape your understanding of God's power and His desire to heal? What new insights have you gained about the nature of miracles and healing processes?

CHAPTER 3

FAITH AND LOVE: IMPORTANT KEYS TO EXPERIENCING DUNAMIS POWER

1 Corinthians 13:13 NKJV"And now abide faith, hope, love, these three; but the greatest of these is love."

In our exploration of how God's healing power operates, it's essential to recognize the significant roles of **Faith and Love** in activating God's dynamic power, or **dunamis**. As we delve deeper into the scriptures and personal experiences, we learn that these two elements must intertwine for the miracle-working power of God to be fully effective. This realization is not just theological—it's practical and can profoundly impact how we conduct our lives and ministries.

Therapeuo Healing, often a process but sometimes instantaneous, illustrates the spectrum of healing practices mentioned in the Bible, which includes laying on of hands, anointing with oil, and the use of healing leaves. This broadens our understanding of how healing can manifest, showing that it can be both a divine instant occurrence and a natural, gradual process. The root word 'therapeuo' gives us the term therapeutic, which implies a process and suggests that healing sometimes requires time, involving various remedies and practices that are both spiritual and physical.

During communal gatherings and personal prayer times, the presence or absence of faith and love can significantly influence the manifestation of healing. It's crucial to create an environment where **Faith and Love** are present, as these are the conduits through which God's power flows most freely. In scenarios where these elements are missing, such as in Jesus' hometown, the scriptures recount that His ability to perform **dunamis miracles** was hindered, although **therapeutic healings** were still possible. This distinction highlights the need for a receptive and open heart, underscored by faith and love, to fully experience God's power.

Moreover, exploring specific **Therapeutic Practices** endorsed by scripture, like fasting, maintaining a cheerful heart, and using a little wine for stomach issues, we see a scriptural basis for embracing a variety of healing practices. These practices not only align with spiritual healing but also emphasize the importance of caring for the body and mind in natural ways, which can enhance or complement divine healing.

The interaction between faith energized by love—what the scriptures describe as faith working through love—shows that **Dunamis Power** is not autonomous; it needs human receptivity and divine love to be fully effective. Where there is skepticism, cynicism, or lack of love, even the potential for divine miracles can be stifled. This understanding pushes us to foster environments where faith and love are not just taught but are vividly lived out and experienced.

By acknowledging the need for environments rich in faith and love, we can better facilitate gatherings where the miraculous can routinely occur. This means intentionally nurturing these virtues within our communities and personal lives, encouraging each other towards deeper faith and more profound expressions of love. In doing so, we align more closely with the biblical model of healing, which is holistic and encompasses both spiritual and physical dimensions.

In summary, the chapter underscores that both **instantaneous miracles** and **process healing** are valid and vital expressions of God's healing power. It invites us to a deeper engagement with our faith, challenges us to love more genuinely, and encourages us to embrace a broader understanding of healing. By doing so, we open ourselves up to the full spectrum of God's healing power, prepared to receive and minister healing in whatever form it may manifest.

REFLECTIVE QUESTIONS

1. How do I cultivate environments in my church and home where faith and love are actively promoted and practiced?
2. In what ways can I personally contribute to increasing faith and love among my community to encourage the flow of God's healing power?
3. How have I experienced the connection between faith and love in my own spiritual walk, and how has it affected my experiences with God's power?
4. What therapeutic practices have I overlooked that could complement my spiritual practices in seeking healing?
5. How can I better integrate the teachings on therapeuo and dunamis in my ministry and personal life to foster a more holistic approach to healing?

- **Cultivate an Environment of Faith and Love**: Work to build a community where faith and love are the foundations of every gathering. Encourage open expressions of faith and acts of love within your community.

- **Equip with Knowledge on Therapeutic Practices**: Educate yourself and your community on the various therapeutic practices mentioned in the Bible. Host seminars or study groups to explore how these can be integrated with spiritual practices for holistic healing.

- **Engage in Faith and Love Practices**: Actively engage in practices that promote both faith and healing, such as prayer meetings focused on deepening faith and communal activities that foster love and unity among believers.

JOURNALING **Prompt**

Reflect on your own experiences where either faith or love was lacking and consider how it might have affected the outcome of a prayer or healing service. How can you personally foster more faith and love in your life to become a conduit for God's power? What steps can you take to ensure these key elements are present in your spiritual practice and community interactions?

CHAPTER 4
GET IN SPIRIT

"Set your mind on things above, not on things on the earth."
- Colossians 3:2 NKJV

In our journey toward deeper spiritual understanding and power, **Being in the Spirit** emerges as a fundamental condition, crucial for tuning into God's frequencies. It is here that we hear His voice, see His visions, and feel His energy pulsating through us, a concept that must be as accessible as breathing, simple enough even for children to grasp and embrace. When we achieve this state, we tap into the divine flow that enables us to perceive and participate in the miraculous.

The scriptures teach us to **Fuel Faith** by listening attentively to what God is saying and observing what He is doing. This engagement with divine communication does more than just sustain our faith—it enlarges it, equipping us to act decisively and boldly in alignment with God's purposes. Similarly, we must **Fuel Love** by perceiving and embodying God's boundless compassion towards everyone. This love is not passive; it is an active, dynamic force that propels God's healing power.

However, many of us face the challenge of the **Western mindset**, which often prioritizes intellectual reasoning over spiritual intuition. This cultural inclination encourages us to live from our minds rather than from our hearts. Yet, the Bible directs us differently, urging us to live and walk by the Spirit. This calls for a significant shift—a transformation that moves us from head to heart, enabling us to live out of a place of spiritual intuition and connectivity.

For those naturally inclined towards intuitive thinking, like the **right-brain individuals**, stepping into this flow may come more naturally. However, this chapter underscores that regardless of our natural predispositions, we can all cultivate the ability to live by the Spirit. This cultivation involves **Practical steps to being in the Spirit**, which include achieving stillness, seeking visions, embracing the flow of thoughts and images from God, and journaling these revelations. These practices are not just exercises; they are gateways to a deeper communion with the divine.

Jesus as our model demonstrated what it means to live continually in the Spirit. He consistently aligned His actions with the visions and words given by His Father, showing us that to walk in power and truth, we must remain in constant dialogue with God. Emulating Jesus means tuning into the Father's voice and vision within (flowing thoughts and flowing pictures). Jesus always did what His Father within was directing Him to do, so the Spirit was never grieved, and power was always available to Jesus. The religious leaders were listening instead to the voice of their father, satan.

As we endeavor to overcome the **cultural and personal barriers** that keep us from a full spiritual walk, we must choose the path of the Spirit with intentionality and practice it until it becomes our natural state. This is not merely about adopting a new way of thinking; it's about embracing a new way of being that permeates every aspect of our lives.

The role of the Holy Spirit in this process cannot be overstated. The Spirit is not just a helper; He is our enabler, the one who breathes life into our spiritual practices and makes the presence of God a tangible reality in our lives. As we learn to lean not on our own understanding but on the promptings and power of the Spirit, we open ourselves to a life of miraculous possibilities.

The ultimate goal is a **Lifestyle of being in the Spirit**. This isn't about occasional spiritual highs or moments of clarity during prayer times; it's about a consistent, daily walk that reflects our deep and abiding connection with God. It's about allowing the Spirit to lead every decision, every interaction, and every moment of our lives.

By embracing these truths and practices, we don't just change individually; we transform our environments. As we model and teach these principles, we help others around us to step into their own spiritual journeys, fostering a community where being in the Spirit is the norm, not the exception. This chapter invites us to embark on this transformative path, promising not just a deeper understanding of God's power but a more profound experience of His presence in every aspect of our lives.

REFLECTIVE QUESTIONS

1. What practical changes can I make to shift from living out of my head to living from my heart?
2. How can I incorporate the practice of stillness and vision into my daily routine to better tune into the Holy Spirit?

3. In what ways have I experienced the flow of divine energy when I have successfully tuned into the Spirit?
4. What barriers in my cultural or personal background may be hindering me from fully embracing a life led by the Spirit?
5. How can I teach and encourage others, especially those new to the faith, to start practicing being in the Spirit?

Actionable Steps

- **Cultivate Stillness:** Set aside daily times of stillness where you quiet your mind and focus on God's presence. Use this time to listen for His voice and sense His guiding impressions.
- **Equip with Scriptural Insights:** Regularly study and meditate on scriptures that emphasize living by the Spirit. Equip yourself and others with knowledge that reinforces the importance of spiritual dependence over reliance on human understanding.
- **Engage in Community Practice:** Organize or participate in community gatherings focused on practicing presence. This could be through group meditations, worship sessions, or spiritual workshops where participants learn to sense and flow in the Spirit together.

JOURNALING Prompt

Reflect on a recent situation where you needed to be in the Spirit but struggled to connect. What were the distractions or barriers? How can you prepare differently in the future to ensure that you are walking in tune with the Spirit, ready to receive and act on God's guidance?

CHAPTER 5

KINGDOM EMOTIONS PRODUCE KINGDOM HEALTH

God has equipped us with the ability to experience and express a range of emotions, and He desires for us to live in the fullness of joy and peace that comes from Him. Embrace the transformative power of Kingdom emotions to enhance your spiritual and physical well-being.

"The joy of the Lord is your strength." - Nehemiah 8:10 (NKJV)

In this chapter, we explore the profound realization that our emotions are not accidental but are **Emotions as Divine Creations** crafted by God Himself. I once believed that emotions were unreliable and should be suppressed, but Scripture and personal reflection have taught me that God created these feelings within us for a purpose. They are meant to enhance our lives, not hinder them. Recognizing this can dramatically transform how we handle our emotional experiences, urging us to manage them responsibly and view them as integral to our spiritual and physical well-being.

Moreover, the Bible teaches us that certain emotions can actively contribute to our health. **Kingdom Emotions Enhance Health** by turning on our immune system and fostering an environment of healing within us. Emotions like joy, peace, love, and gratitude are not just pleasant feelings but are crucial for maintaining good health. This realization encourages us to cultivate such emotions actively, understanding their role not only in spiritual growth but also in physical health management.

A pivotal aspect of maintaining health through emotions is the act of forgiveness. **The Role of Forgiveness in Health** is significant, as unforgiveness is often linked to physical ailments. Holding onto grudges can cause immense stress, leading to actual health problems. Forgiving others, as well as ourselves, is not merely a moral or spiritual duty but a health necessity. It's about releasing that stress and allowing our bodies and spirits to heal.

The Scriptures provide numerous examples that highlight the link between emotional distress and physical ailments. **Biblical Integration of Emotions and Health** shows us through characters like Job and David how turmoil and distress can lead to physical suffering. These biblical accounts are not just historical or spiritual lessons but practical insights into how our emotional states directly affect our physical health.

Sin and guilt can have a tangible impact on our bodies, leading to sickness and pain. The Bible makes it clear that **Sin, Guilt, and Health** are interconnected. For instance, David speaks of his bones wasting away due to his iniquities. This teaches us that our spiritual missteps and the guilt they bring can manifest as physical symptoms, reaffirming the need for spiritual cleanliness not just for our souls' sake but for our bodies' as well.

Living according to the Spirit and nurturing the fruit of the Spirit such as love, joy, peace, and patience are essential for health. **Spiritual Fruit Over Fleshly Desires** promotes an environment within us that is conducive to healing and health. Conversely, living in the flesh can lead to destructive emotional states that harm our physical health. It becomes clear then that our spiritual practices and disciplines play a critical role in managing our emotional well-being.

Emotions Affect the Immune System in ways that are profound and often underestimated. Positive emotions can stimulate immune response, whereas negative emotions can suppress it. Understanding this biological connection motivates us to foster positive emotions actively through our thoughts, actions, and prayer life, ensuring our bodies remain resilient against illnesses.

Scripture provides us with a unique perspective on managing our emotional health through visualization. **Visualizations and Emotional Health** are linked as the Bible encourages us to picture wholesome and Christ-centered scenarios. This practice can steer us away from harmful emotions and maintain our spiritual and emotional health. We are taught to visualize scenarios where Christ is present, which helps align our emotions with the divine.

The journey towards emotional health is ongoing and requires continuous effort. **Continuous Emotional Maintenance** through practices such as journaling, spiritual counseling, and introspection is crucial. It's about regularly checking in with ourselves and the Holy Spirit to ensure that our hearts and minds are aligned with God's will.

REFLECTIVE QUESTIONS

1. How have you experienced the impact of both positive and negative emotions on your physical health in the past?
2. In what ways can you actively practice forgiveness in your life to improve both your emotional and physical well-being?
3. Reflect on a time when you felt overwhelmed by negative emotions. How did you handle it, and what could you have done differently based on this chapter's teachings?
4. How does the idea of emotions affecting your immune system change your view on handling stress and emotional distress?
5. Consider the role of joy and peace in your life. How can you more consciously incorporate these Kingdom emotions into your daily routine?

ACTIONABLE STEPS

- **Cultivate Forgiveness**: Begin by identifying any unresolved conflicts or harbored resentments. Set a daily reminder to reflect on these issues, praying for the strength to forgive and release any bitterness.
- **Equip with Scripture**: Memorize and meditate on scriptures related to joy, peace, and love, such as Galatians 5:22-23. Use these verses as a foundation when facing emotional challenges.
- **Engage in Emotional Cleansing**: Schedule regular times for emotional self-examination through

journaling or counseling. Use these sessions to address and process emotional disturbances guided by biblical truths.

31

Journaling Prompt

Reflect on the current state of your emotional health. Are there areas where negative emotions have taken hold? How can you apply the principles from this chapter to move towards healing and embody the Kingdom emotions of joy and peace daily?

CHAPTER 6

RELATIONAL FIVE-STEP PRAYER MODEL BY JOHN WIMBER

Embrace the power of heart-level prayers and experience how they can transform not only your spiritual life but also bring healing and restoration. Trust in the Lord's power to heal and be renewed as you engage deeply with His Spirit through prayer.

"Therefore I say to you, whatever things you ask when you pray, believe that you receive them, and you will have them."
- Mark 11:24 NKJV

In this chapter, we explore the profound depths of **Heart-Level Prayers** which use the language of the heart—thoughts, images, and emotions—to connect deeply with God's Spirit. These types of prayers allow us to transcend mere words, engaging our entire being in a spiritual dialogue that promotes profound healing and understanding. As we delve into this transformative approach, we realize the importance of flowing thoughts and images which are not just mental activities but channels through which the Holy Spirit speaks to us.

Forgiveness as a Foundation for Healing emerges as a

central theme in effective prayer. Through personal experience and guidance from the Scriptures, I have learned that forgiveness is not merely an emotional release but a spiritual command that unlocks divine pathways of healing and restoration. When we forgive, we release not only the burdens of our hearts but also the physical afflictions often tied to these spiritual wounds. This practice is fundamental, whether it's forgiving others, ourselves, or releasing perceived grievances against God, to pave the way for holistic healing.

The power of **Visualizing Healing** during prayer cannot be overstated. This technique involves picturing the person or situation that caused us hurt and then imaginatively placing Christ within that scenario. This method not only helps in transforming our internal wounds but also empowers us to see our situations from a perspective where Christ's redemptive power prevails. It's about re-framing our experiences with the presence of Jesus, ensuring that each prayer reaches the heart level and brings about spiritual and emotional healing.

The **Flow of the Holy Spirit** is essential in recognizing and following the divine guidance that comes during prayer. By staying attuned to this flow—through images, thoughts, and sensations—we align ourselves more closely with God's will and learn to respond more intuitively to His directions during prayer. This sensitivity enhances our ability to pray effectively, not only for ourselves but also when interceding for others.

In the journey of prayer, the emphasis on **Commanding Faith** is crucial. We are taught that heart faith involves not only believing in the heart but also seeing with the eyes of the heart—the outcomes we pray for as already fulfilled. This form of faith is active and dynamic, commanding healing and deliverance with the authority given to us through Christ.

A significant insight from this chapter is the necessity to address prayers at the **Point of Hurt**. Identifying the exact point of emotional or spiritual injury and targeting it in prayer ensures that our intercessions are precise and potent. This might mean visualizing oneself at the moment a generational curse took hold or the instance of a traumatic event, and seeing Christ intervening right at that critical juncture.

Moreover, it's vital to **Engage All Senses** in the process of healing prayer. By involving the client's heart and bodily sensations, we facilitate a full-bodied experience of God's healing power. This engagement helps the individual fully experience what God is doing within and around them, making the prayer session more impactful and transformative.

Prayer as Dialogue is another aspect that we focus on in this chapter. By making prayer an interactive experience where the client reports back their feelings and sensations, the prayer session becomes a two-way conversation that is more responsive and attuned to the needs of the individual.

We also integrate various **Integrative Healing Approaches** in our prayer sessions. Combining different strategies—such as inner healing, deliverance, and physical healing declarations—addresses the complex nature of human afflictions, ensuring a comprehensive approach to healing that considers emotional, spiritual, and physical dimensions.

Finally, the importance of **Post-Prayer Guidance** is highlighted. After a prayer session, providing clients with spiritual and practical advice helps them maintain the healing and deliverance they've received. This guidance is crucial for helping individuals apply their spiritual insights into their daily lives, ensuring long-term transformation and health.

REFLECTIVE QUESTIONS

1. Reflect on a time when you experienced the flow of the Holy Spirit during prayer. What were the signs that indicated His presence?
2. How has forgiveness impacted your spiritual and physical health in the past?
3. Can you recall a prayer experience where visualizing Christ's intervention transformed your emotional state?
4. How do you incorporate the language of the heart in your daily prayers?
5. What steps can you take to enhance your sensitivity to the Holy Spirit's guidance during prayer?

ACTIONABLE STEPS

- **Cultivate a Forgiving Heart**: Identify someone you need to forgive and spend time praying for the strength to forgive them fully. Use visualization techniques to see yourself offering forgiveness in the presence of Christ.
- **Equip with Visualization Techniques**: Practice visualizing healing scenarios daily. Focus on a specific area where you seek healing, and imagine Christ's light and life entering and restoring that part of your life.
- **Engage in Heart-Level Prayer Regularly**: Set aside time each day to engage in prayer that utilizes the language of the heart. Focus on allowing thoughts,

images, and emotions to flow naturally as you seek a deeper connection with God.

Journaling Prompt

Reflect on your current prayer practices. How often do you engage in heart-level prayer that incorporates visualization, forgiveness, and the flow of the Holy Spirit? What changes can you make to deepen your prayer life and enhance your spiritual well-being?

~

CHAPTER 7

WORDS OF KNOWLEDGE INCREASE THE FAITH LEVEL

As you step into the ministry of words of knowledge, remember that each step taken in faith is accompanied by God's grace. Trust in His power to work through you as you reach out to others with His words of healing and encouragement.

"Beloved, do not believe every spirit, but test the spirits, whether they are of God; because many false prophets have gone out into the world." - 1 John 4:1 NKJV

In this exploration of spiritual gifts, particularly the **Purpose and Impact of Words of Knowledge**, we uncover how these divine revelations serve not just to inform but to actively enhance the faith of those receiving healing. When a specific ailment is prophetically identified, it not only validates the presence and power of God among us but also galvanizes the faith of the afflicted, often precipitating instantaneous healing. This dynamic illustrates the profound connection between divine knowledge and human response, which can lead to miraculous recoveries even without direct prayer.

As we delve deeper into how we might **Receive Words of Knowledge**, it becomes clear that the Holy Spirit can alert us to the needs of others through various means. Whether it is a sudden pain that mirrors another's ailment, a vivid picture, or a spontaneous word that flashes across our mind, each of these experiences is a potential revelation from God concerning someone's need for healing. Learning to recognize and trust these impressions is crucial for effectively ministering to those in need.

The way we **Deliver Words of Knowledge** requires a gentle balance of confidence and humility. Recognizing that our reception of God's messages is not infallible, we must approach this service with a heart of humility, offering what we perceive as merely a possibility rather than a certainty. This approach respects the recipient's agency and underscores the exploratory nature of prophetic ministry, inviting them to claim the word if it resonates with their condition.

The Role of Faith in Healing is central to the effectiveness of words of knowledge. It is faith that activates these prophetic insights and translates them into physical healing. Encouraging individuals to step forward in faith, in response to a word of knowledge, aligns them more closely with the potential for God's miraculous intervention in their lives.

Addressing **Practical Aspects of Healing Ministry**, we are reminded of the importance of conducting ourselves with propriety and sensitivity, especially when physical touch is involved in prayer. Ensuring comfort and appropriateness, particularly with members of the opposite sex, reinforces the sanctity and respect inherent in the healing process.

Navigating the **Ethics and Responsibility in Prophecy** involves a continuous learning curve where humility plays a vital role. We are reminded that prophecy and words of knowledge, while powerful, require a careful and respectful delivery, acknowledging our fallibility as human conduits of divine messages.

The benefits of **Community Learning in Prophetic Ministry** cannot be overstated. Engaging with a community provides not only support and feedback but also a rich environment for growth and refinement of one's prophetic abilities. As we interact and learn from others, our own skills are honed and our errors corrected, fostering a collective growth that is both healthy and necessary.

Continuous Improvement and Mastery in the prophetic gifts is a journey of dedication and practice. By setting clear intentions, seeking out mentorship, and engaging in regular practice, we develop a robust proficiency in using these spiritual tools effectively and sensitively.

Vision and Intention in Ministry serve as the compass that guides our actions and decisions in the prophetic realm. By maintaining a clear vision of what we are called to do and continuously aligning our actions with this vision, we ensure that our ministry remains focused and effective.

Lastly, the **Anointing in Prophetic Ministry** is what empowers and validates our efforts. Seeking and recognizing God's anointing in our work ensures that what we do is not only effective but also divinely sanctioned.

Reflective Questions

1. How have you experienced or witnessed the impact of a word of knowledge in a healing service?
2. What are some ways you can cultivate sensitivity to the Holy Spirit to receive words of knowledge?
3. How can you ensure that you deliver words of

knowledge with humility and sensitivity to the recipients' needs?

4. In what ways can community involvement enhance your ability to operate in prophetic gifts?

5. What steps can you take to continually improve and master the skills necessary for effective prophetic ministry?

ACTIONABLE STEPS

- **Cultivate Sensitivity to the Holy Spirit**: Regularly set aside time for prayer and meditation to enhance your sensitivity to the Holy Spirit's guidance. Practice discerning His voice through journaling or small group discussions.

- **Equip with Knowledge and Skills**: Engage in workshops or training sessions on prophetic ministry to learn from experienced leaders. Focus on understanding the biblical foundation of prophecy and practical aspects of delivering words of knowledge.

- **Engage in Community Learning**: Participate in a prophetic community or support group where you can practice, receive feedback, and grow in your prophetic gifting. This community should be a safe space for learning and mutual encouragement.

Journaling **Prompt**

Reflect on your current practice in the ministry of words of knowledge. Consider your experiences of receiving, interpreting, and delivering these words. What challenges have you faced, and how have you addressed them? What is God teaching you through these experiences?

CHAPTER 8

PRACTICAL GUIDELINES AS WE MINISTER HEALING

Healing ministry is a beautiful partnership with God, where we become vessels of His love and power. Remember that the process of healing flows from God's heart through our willing hands and compassionate spirits. Trust in His faithfulness as you step into this sacred calling, knowing that His love transforms lives and brings wholeness.

"But the path of the just is like the shining sun, that shines ever brighter unto the perfect day." - Proverbs 4:18 NKJV

In this chapter, I want to share **Practical Steps for Ministering Healing** that are rooted in biblical, spiritual, and actionable practices. Healing ministry begins with **Healing Rooted in Love.** True healing flows from unconditional love. When we approach others with genuine care and compassion, we create an atmosphere where God's healing power can move freely. It is not just about the techniques we use but the posture of our hearts as we minister.

One of the most significant barriers to healing is **Over-**

coming Doubt and Fear. Fear, doubt, and disbelief can hinder the flow of God's power, whether in the one ministering or the one receiving healing. These obstacles must be addressed and overcome through prayer and trust in God's promises. Doubt dissipates when we anchor ourselves in His Word and His faithfulness.

As we engage in healing ministry, **Joy, Gratitude, and Love as Healing Emotions** play a transformative role. Emotions such as joy and gratitude not only align us with God's Spirit but also enhance the atmosphere for miracles to occur. Healing becomes more effective when we cultivate these emotions in ourselves and encourage them in others.

A critical aspect of this ministry is **Tuning to the Spirit**. It is essential to take a moment to quiet ourselves and connect with the Holy Spirit. By tuning in to His flowing thoughts, visions, and sensations, we align with His leading, which guides our actions and prayers. This connection allows us to minister effectively, hearing and seeing what God is doing in the moment.

Ministering healing also requires that we learn the discipline of **Living in the Spirit**. This involves stepping away from the distractions of the flesh, including ego, fear, and personal agendas, and instead abiding in Christ. Through practice and continual focus on His presence, we can cultivate a lifestyle of living and walking by the Spirit.

The Power of Visualization is another key element of effective healing ministry. Pictures can increase faith and unlock miracle-working power. Visualizing Jesus at work, whether healing a wound or filling a room with His light, strengthens our confidence in His ability to transform situations. These images anchor our prayers in faith and align them with God's promises.

When we engage in **Group Soaking Prayer**, we tap into the multiplied anointing that comes from corporate prayer. Unity and love among believers amplify the flow of God's Spirit, bringing profound healing and restoration. Group prayer allows us to witness God's power moving through a collective act of faith and agreement.

To maximize the effectiveness of our ministry, we must identify and address **Unbiblical Beliefs** that hinder healing. False beliefs such as "I am unworthy" or "This illness is my punishment" must be replaced with God's truth. Healing cannot flow freely when we are bound by lies that contradict His Word. By repenting of these beliefs and embracing His promises, we unlock the full potential of His healing power.

Deliverance as Part of Healing is often necessary, as many illnesses and emotional wounds are linked to spiritual oppression. Jesus frequently combined deliverance with healing, and we are called to do the same. Repentance removes the legal rights of the enemy, paving the way for freedom and restoration.

Finally, practical guidelines ensure our ministry is Spirit-led and effective. These **Practical Steps for Ministering Healing** include asking permission to pray, being specific in our prayers, and observing what God is doing as the healing unfolds. Staying attuned to His presence allows us to partner with Him in bringing miracles to completion.

These principles are not merely theoretical. They are rooted in Scripture and designed to equip you to step boldly into the ministry of healing, empowered by His Spirit and guided by His love. Through these practical steps, you can become a vessel of God's healing power, transforming lives and glorifying His name.

REFLECTIVE QUESTIONS

1. What steps can you take to ensure your healing ministry is rooted in unconditional love and compassion?

2. How can you overcome fear, doubt, or disbelief in your life and ministry?

3. Reflect on a time when joy or gratitude played a significant role in your spiritual journey. How can these emotions influence your healing ministry?

4. What practices help you tune into the Spirit and quiet your flesh?

5. How do you identify and replace unbiblical beliefs that may hinder healing?

ACTIONABLE STEPS

- **Cultivate Emotional Alignment with God's Love**: Spend time in prayer, asking God to fill your heart with joy, gratitude, and compassion. Let these emotions flow naturally as you prepare to minister healing.

- **Equip Yourself with Scriptural Foundations**: Memorize and meditate on key Bible passages about healing and deliverance to strengthen your faith and guide your ministry.

- **Engage in Group Soaking Prayer**: Join or lead a group prayer session focused on healing, emphasizing unity, mutual love, and listening to God's guidance.

JOURNALING Prompt

Reflect on your current practices in ministering healing. How do you align your actions with God's unconditional love? Are there fears or beliefs you need to confront and replace? What steps can you take to strengthen your connection to the Spirit in your healing ministry?

~

CHAPTER 9

PEG YARBROUGH'S SPIRIT-LED APPROACH TO HEALING

Healing is a deeply personal and transformative experience that involves inviting the presence of Jesus into every aspect of our hearts and lives. The Spirit-led approach to healing reminds us that no two situations are the same, and through trust, patience, and openness, God works uniquely in every individual. Allow the Holy Spirit to guide you as you minister healing to others or seek it for yourself, knowing that His presence brings light, truth, and wholeness.

"And the power of the Lord was present to heal them." – Luke 5:17 NKJV

Rev. Peg Yarbrough's **Spirit-Led Healing Approach** is a testament to the principles we've explored in this journey, showing how God meets each person in their unique needs. Peg emphasizes that **Healing is Rooted in Love.** Every session begins with prayer, asking Jesus to fill the hearts of all involved and to provide a hedge of protection. This atmosphere of unconditional love creates the foundation for trust and openness, essential for the healing process.

Trust plays a critical role in this ministry. Peg describes **Building Trust** as a step where she seeks Jesus' guidance to help the individual feel safe and open. This process involves specific questions that uncover the heart's needs and desires. In larger meetings, the atmosphere of faith may allow for quick healings, but in one-on-one sessions, trust-building often requires time and sensitivity.

Healing often unfolds like **Peeling an Onion**. Rarely is it a single issue but rather layers of body, soul, and spirit concerns. Peg's approach recognizes the need for multiple sessions to address past traumas, generational curses, word curses, and soul ties. Jesus is always at the center of these sessions, acting as the great Counselor. By asking Spirit-led questions, Peg allows Jesus to minister directly to the client's heart, leading to revelations that would otherwise remain hidden.

A key principle is to **Let Jesus Do the Counseling**. Peg encourages her clients to envision Jesus in a safe, loving place and share what He is speaking. This flow of divine communication is transformative. By inviting Jesus to fill the spaces vacated by negative energy or lies, the client experiences profound light and healing.

Through this process, it becomes evident that **Patience is Crucial**. Peg has learned not to rush the work of Jesus, even when sessions feel unproductive initially. Often, breakthrough comes unexpectedly, like pieces of a puzzle suddenly coming together. The joy and relief on the client's face are undeniable confirmations of God's touch.

Uncovering Lies That Block Healing is another essential aspect of Peg's ministry. Lies such as "I don't trust God" or "I'm not good enough" hinder the flow of dunamis power. Identifying and replacing these lies with God's truth allows healing to flow freely. Similarly, **Overcoming Emotional Blocks** such as shame, guilt, and fear opens the heart to receive the fullness of God's love and restoration.

Peg's approach also addresses **Repressed Memories** that restrict healing. Traumatic events often lie at the root of major illnesses. By bringing these memories to the surface and inviting Jesus into those moments, the client experiences deep, lasting healing. Peg emphasizes that true healing requires addressing the root cause and lies that perpetuate the cycle of pain.

Finally, Peg reminds us that **Healing Is Proclaiming the Kingdom**. Just as Jesus sent His disciples to heal the sick and cast out demons, every act of healing is a declaration of God's reign. Through Spirit-led prayer and ministry, we not only restore individuals but also advance the Kingdom of God.

This approach calls for faith, sensitivity, and a willingness to let Jesus lead every step. It is a privilege to participate in His healing work and witness the miraculous transformation in people's lives.

REFLECTIVE QUESTIONS

1. How can you incorporate trust-building into your approach to ministering healing?
2. What lies or emotional blocks might be hindering you or others from receiving God's healing power?
3. How can you ensure that Jesus remains at the center of your healing ministry?
4. What does it mean to you that healing is a proclamation of the Kingdom of God?
5. In what ways can you grow in patience and sensitivity when ministering to others?

· · ·

ACTIONABLE STEPS

- **Cultivate Trust in Jesus' Presence**: Begin each healing session with a heartfelt prayer, asking for Jesus' guidance and protection. Let love and compassion guide your interactions.
- **Equip Yourself to Identify Lies and Blocks**: Study Scripture and ask the Holy Spirit for discernment to uncover limiting beliefs or repressed memories that hinder healing.
- **Engage in Spirit-Led Ministry**: Create space for the Holy Spirit to move by asking open-ended questions and allowing Jesus to minister directly to the person's heart.

JOURNALING Prompt

Lord, how can I grow in sensitivity to Your Spirit in the ministry of healing? What specific steps would You have me take to address lies, emotions, or memories that block the flow of Your healing power? Show me how to trust Your timing and be a vessel of Your love and restoration.

CHAPTER 10

A SPIRIT-LED PROTOCOL FOR CLAIMING GOD'S PROMISES

Trusting in God's promises is not about mechanical repetition or forcing outcomes but about walking in intimacy with the One who made the promise. As we tune our hearts to God, we find assurance that His word will never fail. His promises, rooted in His character, are more certain than the ground we stand on. Trust Him to guide you, speak to you, and lead you into the fullness of His blessings.

For all the promises of God in Him are Yes, and in Him Amen, to the glory of God through us. 2 Corinthians 1:20

Claiming God's promises is a journey of intimacy, trust, and active faith. It begins with the understanding that **faith must start with a spoken word from the Lord.** God's promises are not randomly plucked from Scripture and mechanically applied; they are rooted in His living word, which speaks directly to our circumstances. Like Abraham, we must first receive a rhema word, a specific and personal promise from God, which serves as the foundation of our faith journey.

Once we have this promise, **God often adds a vision, a picture of the promise fulfilled**, to strengthen our belief. Abraham saw the stars in the sky as a representation of the countless descendants God promised him. This vision turned an abstract promise into a tangible reality. Similarly, we should ask God to show us what His promises look like in our lives. These Spirit-given images fill our hearts with hope and align our minds with His plans.

Next, we must **choose to ponder God's promises and visions and reject doubt**. Abraham did not waver in unbelief when faced with the impossibilities of his aged body and Sarah's barrenness. Instead, he gave glory to God, focusing solely on His promise. This teaches us to guard our thoughts and meditate on God's word and visions rather than the obstacles before us. Whatever we fix our eyes upon grows within us, so we must fix them firmly on Jesus and His promises.

Faith becomes active when we **speak God's promises as He directs**. Abraham's new name, meaning "father of many nations," was a declaration of the promise God gave him. Each time he introduced himself, he was proclaiming God's word over his life. Our words hold power when they are aligned with God's revelation, shaping the reality of His promises in our lives.

Faith also requires action. **Obedience to God's instructions demonstrates our trust in Him**. When God told Abraham to circumcise his household, he acted immediately, even though the promise of a son had not yet been fulfilled. Obedience, no matter how small or challenging, opens the door for God's blessings to manifest. We, too, must act on His instructions, stepping out in faith while trusting Him to guide our steps.

It is crucial to **die to self-effort and surrender to God's timing**. Abraham and Sarah waited twenty-four years for Isaac's birth, teaching us the importance of patience and reliance on God. Attempting to fulfill God's promises through human effort leads to disappointment and unintended consequences, as seen with Ishmael. True faith rests in God's perfect plan, trusting that He will fulfill His promises at the appointed time.

Finally, we must trust that **God will bring forth the miracle in His fullness of time**. Sarah's pregnancy and Isaac's birth came exactly when God had ordained. His timing is often beyond our understanding, but it is always perfect. While we wait, we remain faithful, continuing to worship and obey Him. This posture of trust and expectation keeps us aligned with His will and prepares us to receive His blessings.

This Spirit-led protocol for claiming God's promises reminds us that it is not about controlling or demanding outcomes but about partnering with God. By listening for His voice, envisioning His promises, meditating on His word, speaking His truth, acting in obedience, and surrendering to His timing, we live out a faith that honors Him and brings His promises to fruition. Faith is not passive but an active, relational journey with the God who fulfills every promise He makes.

REFLECTIVE QUESTIONS

1. How can I recognize the rhema word God is speaking to me in my current circumstances?
2. What vision has God given me that helps me understand His promises for my life?
3. How can I remain steadfast in pondering God's promises rather than focusing on obstacles?
4. What specific steps of obedience is God calling me to take today as an act of faith?
5. How can I cultivate patience and trust in God's timing for His promises to manifest?

. . .

ACTIONABLE STEPS

- **Cultivate** a heart of intimacy by spending daily time in prayer and asking the Holy Spirit to reveal God's promises for your life.
- **Equip** yourself with faith by journaling the visions and words God has given you, allowing them to strengthen your belief and guide your actions.
- **Engage** in obedience by taking specific steps that align with the rhema word and vision God has shown you, trusting Him fully in the process.

JOURNALING **Prompt**

Ask the Lord, "What specific promise are You highlighting for my life today? How can I align my thoughts, words, and actions with this promise to see it fulfilled in Your perfect timing?" Write down the vision He shows you and the steps He directs you to take.

~

CHAPTER II

TWENTY-EIGHT THERAPEUTIC HEALING PROTOCOLS

Healing is not only about restoring the body but also about aligning the mind, spirit, and emotions with God's design. God, in His infinite wisdom, has provided natural and spiritual resources for our healing. When we embrace His promises and apply His principles, we step into a life of wholeness and freedom. No matter the struggle, there is always hope, as God's power and guidance are ever-present.

Bless the Lord, O my soul, and forget not all His benefits: who forgives all your iniquities, who heals all your diseases, who redeems your life from destruction, who crowns you with lovingkindness and tender mercies. (Psalm 103:2–4 NKJV)

The journey of healing is a dynamic relationship between God's divine provisions, our faith, and our actions. **God's design for self-healing is evident in the way our bodies work to restore themselves when nurtured with emotional peace, proper nutrition, and rest. A**

67

simple cut on the skin begins to heal without our intervention. This inherent ability reflects God's intent for health and wellness. To align with this design, we must provide our bodies with the right tools, including physical care and emotional stability.

Healing often begins in the spiritual realm. **Casting out demons, as modeled by Jesus, demonstrates that spiritual oppression can affect physical health.** Deliverance brings release and restoration, opening the door to wholeness. Similarly, **breaking generational curses allows us to step into freedom, leaving behind inherited struggles and embracing God's blessings.** In prayer, we place the cross of Christ between us and past patterns, inviting the blessings of Calvary to flow into our lives.

Releasing residual trauma from our bodies is another essential step in the healing process. By commanding the memories of trauma to leave in Jesus' name, we align our physical and spiritual health. This practice works alongside **God's provision in herbs and natural remedies, which Scripture affirms are given for the healing of nations.** From biblical examples of bitter water made sweet to the modern use of herbal remedies, God's gifts in nature are a powerful resource for health.

Healing encompasses the whole person, including emotional well-being. **Emotional wholeness is a critical component of health, as joy, gratitude, and forgiveness can displace the negative emotions of fear, anger, and hopelessness.** Our emotional state influences our physical health, making practices such as laughter and worship vital for wellness. **Praise and worship invite God's presence, which strengthens both the spirit and body.** Worshiping the Lord brings peace, reduces stress, and revitalizes the soul.

Practical habits play a significant role in maintaining health. **A healthy diet, proper hydration, and sufficient rest are foun-**

dational to physical well-being. These practices honor our bodies as temples of the Holy Spirit, creating an environment conducive to healing. Tools such as anointing with oil and confessing sins connect the spiritual and physical aspects of health, ensuring that we address the root causes of illness.

Speaking life over oneself in alignment with God's promises is a declaration of faith that activates healing. Words carry power, shaping our realities and creating an atmosphere for miracles. This authority extends to engaging in exercise, using therapeutic remedies like chiropractic care, and finding peace through soaking prayer. As we apply these principles, we step into the abundant life God promises, trusting Him to bring health and wholeness.

God's healing plan is both practical and spiritual. By embracing these therapeutic protocols, we align ourselves with His will, stepping into the fullness of life and health He desires for us. Healing is not just about the absence of illness but the presence of His abundant grace at work within us.

REFLECTIVE QUESTIONS

1. **What steps can I take to align my life with God's design for healing?** Reflect on physical, emotional, and spiritual aspects of your well-being.

2. **How can I apply the practice of speaking life over my body and circumstances?** Consider specific areas where you can replace negative words with God's promises.

3. **What role does emotional wholeness play in my overall health?** Identify areas of fear, anger, or hopelessness that need to be replaced with joy and forgiveness.

4. **Are there any natural remedies or therapeutic practices I can incorporate into my healing journey?** Seek God's guidance in exploring His provision through nature.

5. **How can praise and worship become a regular part of my healing process?** Reflect on ways to invite God's presence into your daily routine.

ACTIONABLE STEPS

- **Cultivate** a daily habit of emotional and spiritual care by meditating on Scripture, praying, and worshiping God to foster joy and peace.
- **Equip** your body with proper nutrition, hydration, and rest to create an environment conducive to healing, using natural remedies as necessary.
- **Engage** in practical faith by speaking life, applying therapeutic practices, and trusting God for complete restoration in every area of your life.

JOURNALING Prompt

Spend time journaling about areas in your life where you need healing, whether physical, emotional, or spiritual. Ask God to reveal any root causes or next steps He wants you to take. Write down any promises or insights He speaks to you.

~

CHAPTER 12

PLANTED BY THE RIVER AND BEARING FRUIT CONTINUALLY

The promise of a life filled with fruitfulness, healing, and divine presence is not only an invitation but a reality for those who remain connected to God's River of Life. No matter the season, He nourishes us, empowers us, and provides a foundation for unshakable peace and joy. We are like trees planted by His rivers, continually yielding fruit and bringing forth healing, reflecting His unchanging faithfulness. This is the life we are called to live —a life of abiding, flowing, and thriving in His Spirit.

"He shall be like a tree planted by the rivers of water, that brings forth its fruit in its season, whose leaf also shall not wither; and whatever he does shall prosper." Psalm 1:3 (NKJV)

The vision of **God's River of Life** flowing from His throne has shaped my understanding of the Spirit-led life. This river brings healing and sustains everything it touches, reminding us that life flourishes in His presence. It is the Holy Spirit's work to make this a living reality for those who trust and abide in Him. I have discovered that **abiding in Christ is the foundation of all fruitfulness,** as Jesus Himself emphasized. This is not a casual relationship but a continual connection, like a branch attached to the vine. Without Him, we can do nothing; with Him, we bear much fruit, reflecting His glory in our lives.

Through the years, I have seen the power of **spiritual laws that govern our walk with God.** These principles—faith, abiding, and obedience—are not burdensome but freeing. They open the door to miraculous provision, guidance, and transformation. When I focus on living in the present moment with the Holy Spirit, I am reminded to still my heart and listen for His voice. This leads to **living moment by moment in His flow**, a life marked by spontaneous thoughts, visions, and peace that only He can provide.

The dynamic nature of **flow is a hallmark of the Spirit-led life**. Just as wind and water move in response to unseen forces, so the Spirit moves through us when we yield to His guidance. This understanding has reshaped how I approach challenges and decisions, aligning my actions with the gentle nudges of His Spirit. As I practice the art of **picturing truth**, I realize the transformative power of envisioning His promises, seeing His presence, and allowing those images to shape my emotions and actions. This practice strengthens my faith and helps me step confidently into His plans.

I have also learned that **speaking life releases God's power,** and this truth has been a guiding principle in my journey. Words carry the power to create or destroy, to heal or harm. When we speak in alignment with God's truth, we partner with Him in releasing His will on earth. This truth is closely tied to the restoration of **communion with God,** which Jesus made possible through His sacrifice. We now have access to the Tree of Life, a symbol of continual fruitfulness and healing.

To sustain this spiritual vitality, I must engage in **daily fellowship with God**. Like gathering manna in the wilderness, this connection must be renewed each day. Yesterday's victories are not enough for today's battles. Each morning, I draw strength and wisdom from His presence, aligning myself with His purposes. Finally, I have seen how **healing flows from spiritual alignment**. When my thoughts, words, and actions are in harmony with His truth, His power moves freely, bringing restoration and wholeness. This is the life He has called us to live —a life planted by His river, bearing fruit continually.

REFLECTIVE QUESTIONS

1. What does being "planted by the river" mean to you, and how does it shape your understanding of spiritual fruitfulness?
2. How can you cultivate a deeper practice of abiding in Christ in your daily life?
3. What are some areas where you need to realign with the spiritual laws of faith, obedience, or flow?
4. How has your perspective on words changed in light of the truth that speaking life releases God's power?
5. What practical steps can you take to ensure that you are experiencing daily fellowship with God and drawing from His presence?

ACTIONABLE STEPS

- **Cultivate** Set aside time daily to practice stillness and abide in God's presence. Use this time to quiet your heart, listen for His voice, and reflect on His promises.

- **Equip** Develop a habit of speaking life-filled words over yourself and others. Be intentional about aligning your speech with God's truth and promises.
- **Engage** Look for opportunities to live in the flow of the Holy Spirit. Respond to His nudges, whether it's in acts of kindness, prayer, or sharing His love with others.

Journaling **Prompt**

Reflect on a time when you experienced the flow of the Holy Spirit in your life. What did it feel like, and how did it shape your understanding of abiding in Christ? Write about ways you can invite His presence to flow more freely in your daily life.

DESTINY IMAGE

Destiny Image is a prophetic Christian publisher dedicated to empowering believers through Spirit-led messages. Our mission is to equip and inspire individuals to fulfill their God-given destinies by providing transformative resources that resonate with the Charismatic and Pentecostal faith.

We specialize in books, blogs, and back cover copies that reflect prophetic insights, dynamic teachings, and testimonies of faith. Our commitment to fostering spiritual growth and kingdom impact makes Destiny Image a beacon for those seeking to deepen their relationship with God and embrace their calling in the power of the Holy Spirit.